W9-AWS-455

WENDY WATSON'S

Frog Went A-Courting

WENDY WATSON'S

Frog Went A-Courting

LOTHROP, LEE & SHEPARD BOOKS

NEW YORK

For Lewis,
always

Illustrations copyright © 1990 by Wendy Watson
Piano arrangement copyright © 1990 by Paul Alan Levi
All rights reserved. No part of this book may be reproduced or utilized in any form or by any means, electronic or mechanical, including photocopying, recording or by any information storage and retrieval system, without permission in writing from the Publisher. Inquiries should be addressed to Lothrop, Lee & Shepard Books, a division of William Morrow & Company, Inc., 105 Madison Avenue, New York, New York 10016. Printed in the United States of America.

First Edition   1 2 3 4 5 6 7 8 9 10

Library of Congress Cataloging in Publication Data
Watson, Wendy. Wendy Watson's Frog went a-courting / by Wendy Watson.
p.   cm. Summary: Presents the well-known folk song about the courtship and marriage of the frog and the mouse. Includes music. ISBN 0-688-06539-2. —ISBN 0-688-06540-6 (lib. bdg.) 1. Folk songs. [1. Folk songs.] I. Frog he would a-wooing go (Folk song) II. Title. III. Title: Frog went a-courting. PZ8.3.W345Fr   1990   782.42162'0268—dc20
89-63022 CIP AC

Frog went a-courting and he did ride,
    Um-hmm,
Frog went a-courting and he did ride,
    Um-hmm.
Frog went a-courting and he did ride
With a sword and pistol by his side,
    Um-hmm, um-hmm, um-hmm.

He rode up to Miss Mouse's hall,
  Um-hmm,
He rode up to Miss Mouse's hall,
  Um-hmm.
He rode up to Miss Mouse's hall,
Loud and lovely he did call,
  Um-hmm, um-hmm, um-hmm.

He said, Miss Mouse, are you within?
   Um-hmm,
He said, Miss Mouse, are you within?
   Um-hmm.
He said, Miss Mouse, are you within?
Yes, kind sir, I sit and spin!
   Um-hmm, um-hmm, um-hmm.

He took Miss Mouse upon his knee,
    Um-hmm,
He took Miss Mouse upon his knee,
    Um-hmm.
He took Miss Mouse upon his knee,
And he said, Miss Mouse, will you marry me?
    Um-hmm, um-hmm, um-hmm.

Oh no, kind sir, I can't do that,
    Um-hmm,
Oh no, kind sir, I can't do that,
    Um-hmm.
Oh no, kind sir, I can't do that
Without consent of Uncle Rat,
    Um-hmm, um-hmm, um-hmm.

Old Uncle Rat he soon came home,
    Um-hmm,
Old Uncle Rat he soon came home,
    Um-hmm.
Old Uncle Rat he soon came home,
Says, Who's been here since I've been gone?
    Um-hmm, um-hmm, um-hmm.

There's been a pretty young gentleman,
    Um-hmm,
There's been a pretty young gentleman,
    Um-hmm.
There's been a pretty young gentleman
Who says he'll marry me if he can,
    Um-hmm, um-hmm, um-hmm.

Uncle Rat laughed and shook his sides,
   Um-hmm,
Uncle Rat laughed and shook his sides,
   Um-hmm.
Uncle Rat laughed and shook his sides
To think his niece would be a bride,
   Um-hmm, um-hmm, um-hmm.

Then Uncle Rat he went to town,
  Um-hmm,
Then Uncle Rat he went to town,
  Um-hmm.
Then Uncle Rat he went to town
To buy Miss Mouse a wedding gown,
  Um-hmm, um-hmm, um-hmm.

Where shall the wedding supper be?
   Um-hmm,
Where shall the wedding supper be?
   Um-hmm.
Where shall the wedding supper be?
Way down yonder in the hollow tree,
   Um-hmm, um-hmm, um-hmm.

What shall the wedding supper be?
   Um-hmm,
What shall the wedding supper be?
   Um-hmm.
What shall the wedding supper be?
Three green beans and a black-eyed pea,
   Um-hmm, um-hmm, um-hmm.

First to come in was Bumblebee,
    Um-hmm,
First to come in was Bumblebee,
    Um-hmm.
First to come in was Bumblebee
With his fiddle on his knee,
    Um-hmm, um-hmm, um-hmm.

The next to come in was Missus Snake,
    Um-hmm,
The next to come in was Missus Snake,
    Um-hmm.
The next to come in was Missus Snake,
Bringing around the wedding cake,
    Um-hmm, um-hmm, um-hmm.

And then here came old Reverend Bug,
　　Um-hmm,
And then here came old Reverend Bug,
　　Um-hmm.
And then here came old Reverend Bug,
He took his seat by the cider jug,
　　Um-hmm, um-hmm, um-hmm.

Next to come in was a little seed-tick,
   Um-hmm,
Next to come in was a little seed-tick,
   Um-hmm.
Next to come in was a little seed-tick,
He ate so much it made him sick,
   Um-hmm, um-hmm, um-hmm.

Then they sent for Doctor Fly,
    Um-hmm,
Then they sent for Doctor Fly,
    Um-hmm.

Then they sent for Doctor Fly,
He said, Young fellow, you almost died,
    Um-hmm, um-hmm,
    Um-hmm.

Late to come was a nimble flea,
    Um-hmm,
Late to come was a nimble flea,
    Um-hmm.
Late to come was a nimble flea,
He danced a jig for the bumblebee,
    Um-hmm, um-hmm, um-hmm.

But then crept in an old bobcat,
    Um-hmm,
But then crept in an old bobcat,
    Um-hmm.
But then crept in an old bobcat,
And he put a stop to all of that!
    Um-hmm, um-hmm, um-hmm.

So that was the end of the wedding day,
    Um-hmm,
So that was the end of the wedding day,
    Um-hmm.
So that was the end of the wedding day,
And now I have no more to say,
    Um-hmm, um-hmm, um-hmm.

Piano arrangement by Paul Alan Levi